Learn About

THE FIVE SENSES

Hearing

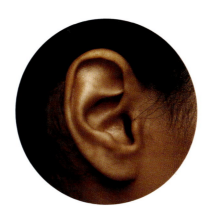

by Claire Caprioli

Children's Press®
An imprint of Scholastic Inc.

Special thanks to our medical content consultant, An Huang, MD, PhD, professor of physiology, New York Medical College.

Library of Congress Cataloging-in-Publication Data
Names: Caprioli, Claire, author.
Title: Hearing / by Claire Caprioli.
Description: First edition. | New York, NY: Children's Press, an imprint of Scholastic Inc., 2024. | Series: Learn about: the five senses | Includes bibliographical references and index. | Audience: Ages 5–7. | Audience: Grades K–1. | Summary: "How do we experience the world? Let's learn all about the five senses! The sense of hearing is one of our five senses. And it is amazing! It helps us carry out a conversation and enjoy music and the sounds of nature. It also warns us if there is danger around. Learn about how we hear, and common problems and diseases connected with it with this perfect first introduction to the sense of hearing! ABOUT THE SERIES: The human body is amazing! It gives us five different ways to learn about the world around us: through the eyes, through the skin, through the tongue, through the ears, and through the nose. Thanks to these parts of our bodies, we can see, feel, taste, hear, and smell. These are the five senses! Why do bananas taste so good? Why does tickling cause so much laughter? Illustrated with familiar examples, this fun nonfiction set in the Learn About series gives readers a close-up look at the five senses, and it teaches them how each of the senses work."— Provided by publisher.
Identifiers: LCCN 2022056758 (print) | LCCN 2022056759 (ebook) | ISBN 9781338898262 (library binding) | ISBN 9781338898279 (paperback) | ISBN 9781338898286 (ebk)
Subjects: LCSH: Hearing—Juvenile literature. | Ear—Juvenile literature. | Senses and sensation—Juvenile literature. | BISAC: JUVENILE NONFICTION / Concepts / Senses & Sensation | JUVENILE NONFICTION / General
Classification: LCC QP462.2 .C355 2024 (print) | LCC QP462.2 (ebook) | DDC 612.8/5—dc23/eng/20230124
LC record available at https://lccn.loc.gov/2022056758
LC ebook record available at https://lccn.loc.gov/2022056759

Copyright © 2024 by Scholastic Inc.

All rights reserved. Published by Children's Press, an imprint of Scholastic Inc., *Publishers since 1920*. SCHOLASTIC, CHILDREN'S PRESS, and associated logos are trademarks and/or registered trademarks of Scholastic Inc.

The publisher does not have any control over and does not assume any responsibility for author or third-party websites or their content.

No part of this publication may be reproduced, stored in a retrieval system, or transmitted in any form or by any means, electronic, mechanical, photocopying, recording, or otherwise, without written permission of the publisher. For information regarding permission, write to Scholastic Inc., Attention: Permissions Department, 557 Broadway, New York, NY 10012.

10 9 8 7 6 5 4 3 2 1   24 25 26 27 28

Printed in China, 62
First edition, 2024

Book design by Kathleen Petelinsek

Photos ©: cover, 1: Jun/Getty Images; 4–5: kali9/Getty Images; 6 left: RyanKing999/Getty Images; 11: severija/Getty Images; 15: Rohappy/Getty Images; 16: andegro4ka/Getty Images; 19: Ariel Skelley/Getty Images; 20: Kittipong Satrinekarn/EyeEm/Getty Images; 23: Hispanolistic/Getty Images; 24: Juan Silva/Getty Images; 27 bottom: andy_Q/Getty Images; 28 top: Harry Zhang/EyeEm/Getty Images; 28 center: NatureLovePhotography/Getty Images; 29 top: Patricia Marroquin/Getty Images; 29 center: Swee Ming Young/Dreamstime; 29 bottom: MRI805/Getty Images; 30 top right: Prostock-Studio/Getty Images; 30 center right: Cavan Images/Getty Images.

All other photos © Shutterstock.

TABLE OF CONTENTS

Did You Hear That? 4
Chapter 1: All Ears 6
Chapter 2: How Do Our Ears Work? 12
Chapter 3: Troubles with Hearing .. 20
Activity: Make an Ear Trumpet 26
Animal Ears 28
Protect Your Hearing! 30
Glossary 31
Index/About the Author 32

INTRODUCTION

Did You Hear That?

Imagine you are telling a knock-knock joke to a friend. Your voices go back and forth. By the end of the joke, you are both giggling. You have both used your sense of hearing to enjoy the joke together.

Hearing is one of the five senses. The other four are sight, smell, taste, and touch. They help us take in information about the world around us.

CHAPTER 1

All Ears

We can hear thanks to our two ears. Hearing helps us communicate. But it does many more things for us! Listen to the sounds around you. Is there music playing or a cat purring? Can you hear whispering or birds chirping?

Our two ears help us tell the direction a sound is coming from and if it is nearby.

Is there a plane flying near you? Our sense of hearing tells us a lot about where we are. It can also keep us safe. For example, if we hear a thunderstorm coming we know we should stay indoors.

Our ears also help us remain steady and upright. This is called balance.

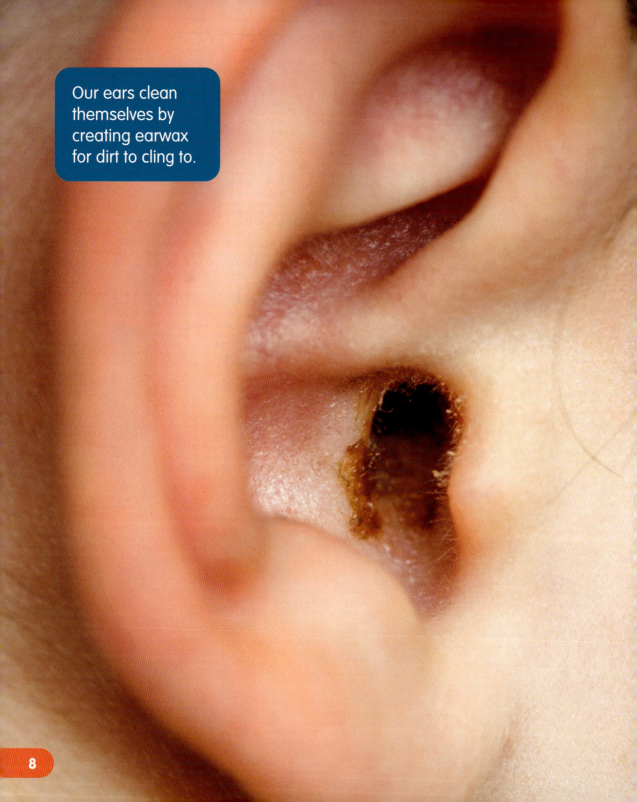

Our ears clean themselves by creating earwax for dirt to cling to.

Earwax is the sticky yellow or brown stuff inside our ears. It may seem gross, but we need earwax! Earwax traps dirt and keeps it from going deep inside the ear. It slowly pushes the dirt back out. Earwax also keeps our ears moist. Without earwax, our ears would be dry, dirty, and itchy!

Earwax is mainly made of dead skin cells.

A sound creates waves. These waves are also called **vibrations**. They are back-and-forth movements in the air. Our ears are able to catch them!

Sounds can be very different. Think about a violin and a bass drum. One of the differences is the **pitch**. The violin has a high pitch. The bass drum has a low pitch.

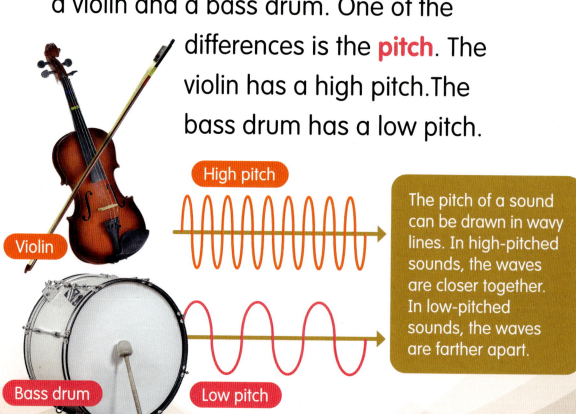

High pitch

Violin

Bass drum

Low pitch

The pitch of a sound can be drawn in wavy lines. In high-pitched sounds, the waves are closer together. In low-pitched sounds, the waves are farther apart.

A stone dropped into a pond makes a wave across the water. Sound works through the air in a similar way.

Sounds travel through the air, liquids, and solids. We can hear someone knocking on a door or shouting underwater.

CHAPTER 2

How Do Our Ears Work?

Check out the different parts of the ear. Most of them are hidden inside our head.

OUTER EAR

PINNA: This is the outside of the ear. We can see two pinnas, one on each side of the head.

EAR CANAL: This small tube sends the sounds toward the eardrum.

EARDRUM: A thin piece of **membrane**. It separates the outer ear from the middle ear.

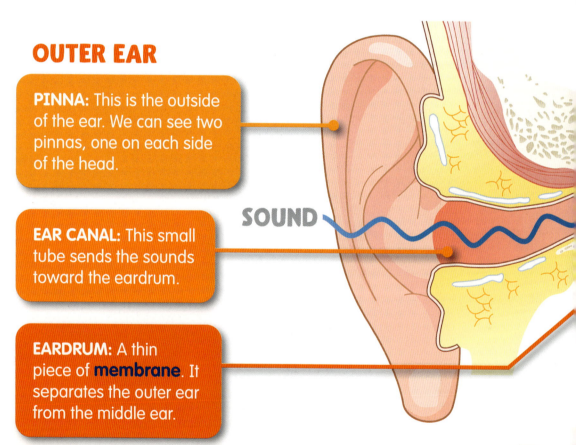

SOUND

MIDDLE EAR

OSSICLES: These are three tiny bones. They are important to hearing.

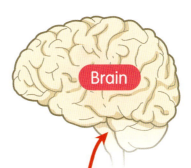

INNER EAR

COCHLEA (KOH-klee-uh): A **cavity** filled with liquid and **sensory** hair cells. It is shaped like a spiral.

EUSTACHIAN (yoo-STAY-shuhn) TUBE: This tube goes between the middle ear and the back of the throat.

AUDITORY NERVE: This nerve sends sound messages to the brain.

SEMICIRCULAR CANALS: These are three liquid-filled loops. They help us keep our balance.

OVAL WINDOW: A thin piece of membrane. It connects the middle ear with the inner ear.

When something around us makes a sound, our pinna catches the vibrations in the air. The pinna acts like a funnel. It moves the sound deeper into the ear. The sound waves go into the ear canal and bounce against the eardrum. Our eardrum works like a drum. Sound waves hit the eardrum and it vibrates.

Our eardrums are about the size of a dime.

Wearing headphones brings sounds closer to our ears. It makes the sounds louder and easier to hear.

The vibrations of the eardrum move into the middle ear. The sound then hits the ossicles. These three little bones are called the malleus (MA-lee-uhs), incus (ING-kuhs), and stapes (STAY-peez). Vibrations travel to the stapes, which knocks against the oval window.

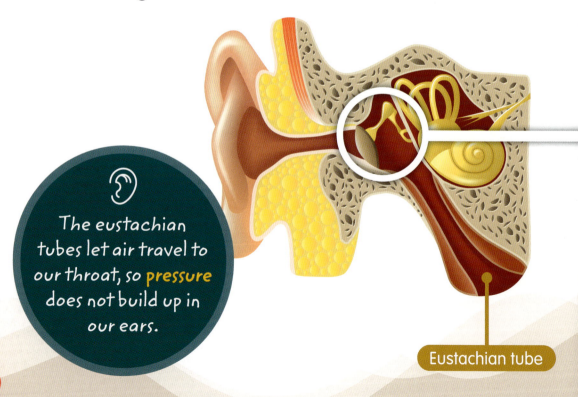

The eustachian tubes let air travel to our throat, so **pressure** does not build up in our ears.

Eustachian tube

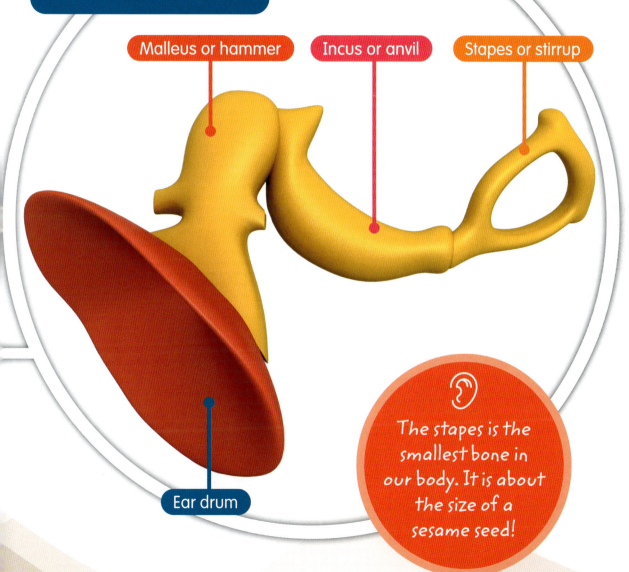

The sound continues its way into the inner ear. The inner ear has a cavity called the cochlea. The cochlea is filled with liquid and sensory hair cells. The sensory hair cells look like little hairs. When the oval window receives the sound waves, the liquid and little hairs in the cochlea move back and forth. The movements send messages to the brain through the auditory nerve. Our brain reads these messages and tells us what we are hearing. We can hear sound!

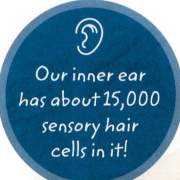

Our inner ear has about 15,000 sensory hair cells in it!

Our brain makes sense of all the sounds we hear in a parade so we can enjoy it!

Swimmer's ear occurs when water stays in the outer ear.

CHAPTER 3

Troubles with Hearing

Sometimes we need help caring for our ears. Then we go to see a special doctor for the ears, nose, and throat. This person is called an ENT doctor.

For example, we can get swimmer's ear after playing in water. Most of the time, water comes out if it has gone into the ear canal. But our ears may hurt if the water doesn't come out. A doctor can give us eardrops. The eardrops dry the water and kill the **bacteria**.

Have you ever had a cold or the flu? With either of them, your eardrum may become red and swollen. You might have an ear **infection**. Ear infections can be painful.

Sometimes ear infections come back often. A doctor may put a tiny ear tube in the eardrum. Ear tubes don't allow **fluid** to build up in the middle ear. They help cure ear infections. They often fall out on their own after a year.

Ear tubes are inserted in the eardrum. They help make our ears feel better.

About one in every 15 children in the United States gets ear tubes by the time they are three years old.

In the United States, people who are deaf or have difficulty hearing—or people who communicate with them—may speak using American Sign Language (ASL).

ASL is becoming a popular second language to learn in high schools and universities across the United States!

Some people do not hear as well as others due to illness or injury or because they are born that way. They may wear hearing aids to help them hear. People who are deaf cannot hear at all. They use their other senses to help them. Some people use hand signals called sign language to communicate.

Hearing aid

We understand sounds thanks to our sense of hearing. Together with the other senses, it keeps us connected to the world around us. What will your senses help you do today?

ACTIVITY: MAKE AN EAR TRUMPET

The first hearing aids were invented more than 300 years ago! They were very simple. People who had trouble hearing would hold a funnel-shaped horn or trumpet up to their ear. This would help direct sounds into their ear. Try it for yourself!

YOU WILL NEED:
- A friend who knows how to snap their fingers
- A piece of heavy paper and tape, or a funnel

STEPS:

1. Roll up the paper to create a funnel, or ice-cream cone shape. Tape it in place.
2. Turn your back to your friend. Ask your friend to take 50 steps away from you.

3 Ask your friend to turn around and snap their fingers.

4 Now, ask them to take a few steps closer and snap again. Ask them to continue doing this until you can hear the snapping. Then ask your friend to mark that spot on the floor.

5 Go back to step 2 and do the activity again, but now listen by using the funnel. Place the small end near your ear (not inside it!) and the wide end toward your friend. Did you hear better with or without the funnel?

WHAT HAPPENED?

You probably were able to hear the snap louder and from farther away when you used the funnel. The funnel acted like a giant ear to catch the sound vibrations and send them into the ear canal. The funnel made the sound louder!

ANIMAL EARS

African Elephant

The Biggest Ears
African elephant ears are the world's largest: 6 feet (2 m) long and 4 feet (1 m) wide! They use their large ears to fan away flies and help keep cool. Elephants can hear sounds that are too low for human ears. They also can communicate over long distances by stamping their feet.

Dolphin

Underwater Listeners
Dolphins make high-pitched sounds underwater. These sound waves bounce back when they hit other objects. The dolphins listen for how the sounds bounce back. This tells them the location and size of the objects around them. This kind of listening is called echolocation. It helps dolphins locate food and stay out of danger.

Townsend Bat

Flying by Ear
Bats also use echolocation. But they use it in the dark, not underwater. Bats make very high-pitched sounds that humans cannot hear. The sounds bounce off objects and return to the bats. Then their large ears pick up the location of the tiny insects they eat.

Feathery Ears

The great horned owl has feather tufts on top of its head. The earholes are hidden underneath. Their right ear is larger than their left and higher up on the head. This helps the owl hear the exact location of its food better.

Strangest Place for Eardrums

The cricket hears like we do, but its eardrums are on its knees! Crickets' two front legs pick up sound vibrations with their eardrums. Their eardrums are some of the tiniest in the animal kingdom.

Waxy Ears

Scientists can tell the age of a whale from the waxy buildup in its ears. A whale's earwax creates a plug in its ears to keep the water out. The wax can also help the whale hear better underwater. In 2007, scientists found a whale that had a 10-inch-long (25 cm) earwax plug. It was as long as three new crayons!

PROTECT YOUR HEARING!

It is important to protect your sense of hearing. Here are a few things you can do!

Always keep the sound low when you listen to music through headphones or earbuds.

Don't put anything in your ears to try to clean them. They will clean themselves!

Always protect your ears from the loud sounds of music, machines, or motorsport events. A pair of earmuffs can help you!

Tilt your head to both sides after you've been swimming or playing in water to let water run out of your ears.

If you wear a hearing aid, your doctor will show you how to take good care of it.

GLOSSARY

bacteria (bak-TEER-ee-uh) microscopic, single-celled living things that exist everywhere and that can either be useful or harmful

cavity (KAV-i-tee) an empty space in something solid

fluid (FLOO-id) a substance that can flow, such as a liquid or a gas

infection (in-FEK-shuhn) an illness caused by bacteria or viruses

membrane (MEM-brane) a very thin layer of tissue that lines or covers certain organs or cells

pitch (PICH) the highness or lowness of a sound

pressure (PRESH-ur) the force produced by pressing on something, as in *blood pressure* or *water pressure*

sensory (SEN-suh-ree) conveying nerve impulses from the sense organs to the nerve centers

vibrations (vye-BRAY-shuhnz) the rapid back and forth movements of something

INDEX

American Sign
    Language (ASL), 24
animals, 28–29
bacteria, 21
balance, 7, 13
cavity, 13, 18
communication, 4–5,
    6, 24–25
deaf people, 24–25
direction of sound, 6
ear, nose, and throat
    (ENT) doctor, 21

ears
  parts of, 12–18
  problems with,
    20–25
  protecting, 30
earwax, 8–9, 29
echolocation, 28
fluid, 22
hearing aids, 25,
    26–27
hearing problems,
    20–25

infection, 22–23
membranes, 12–13
pitch, 10, 28
pressure, 16
safety, 7
sensory hair cells, 13, 18
sign language, 24–25
sound waves, 10–11,
    14–18, 28
swimmer's ear, 20–21
vibrations, 10–11, 14–18,
    27, 29

ABOUT THE AUTHOR

Claire Caprioli is a children's author. She loves reading, learning, exploring nature, and spending lots of time with her family. Her favorite sound is a baby's belly laugh! You can learn more about her at www.clairecaprioli.com.